> We admitted we were powerless over alcohol—that our lives had become unmanageable.
>
> —*Step One*

INTRODUCTION

The **First Step** is where what was impossible starts to become possible. We learn that we can stop drinking or using other drugs one day at a time, that we're not bad people, and that we don't have to be alone anymore. For people with addiction, also called substance use disorder, the First Step is where the miracle of recovery begins.

Step One is the essential key that unlocks the door to sobriety. It gives us a choice. We can remain in our addiction, or we can walk through to a new life that begins with Step One and enlarges to encompass the remaining Steps, because we need all Twelve Steps to fully claim long-term abstinence and recovery.

This pamphlet examines these parts of Step One:

- **The first word,** page 2
- **"Our lives had become unmanageable,"** page 5
- **"We were powerless,"** page 8
- **And so we admitted . . . ,** page 11

Over the days, weeks, months, years, or decades of recovery from substance use disorder, we will need to take the First Step many times, going back to it regularly to remind ourselves that we have a disease of the brain, how we've stayed in recovery, and what's at stake if we return to use. Step One is our bedrock.

The First Word

It all begins with "we."

This first word of the First Step is the key to our recovery. No other word in any of the Steps, in any Twelve Step program, is more important.

On our own, all by ourselves, we tried to stop drinking or using other drugs. We believed that if we tried hard enough, our willpower would keep us sober. When it didn't, we tried again on our own, desperately grasping for an escape from the grip of alcohol or other addictive substances.

Some people can stop drinking or using other drugs, and stay sober all by themselves. They can rely on their solitary "me." We can't.

Even though we live in a world full of other human beings, most of us with substance use disorder can be very lonely people. Our disease overwhelms us, crowding out the people we love, our friends, our coworkers—virtually anyone who might come between us and our drinking or using.

Step One

ADMITTING POWERLESSNESS

This pamphlet discusses AA's Step One, "We admitted we were powerless over alcohol—that our lives had become unmanageable." This admission is the foundation of recovery, but it's something we can't do alone.

Hazelden Publishing
Center City, Minnesota 55012-0176
hazelden.org/bookstore

©2022 by Hazelden Betty Ford Foundation
All rights reserved. Published 2022. (First published digitally in 2021.)
Printed in the United States of America.

No part of this publication, neither print nor electronic, may be reproduced in any form or by any means without the express written permission of the publisher. Failure to comply with these terms may expose you to legal action and damages for copyright infringement.

The Twelve Steps are reprinted with permission of Alcoholics Anonymous World Services, Inc. Permission to reprint the Twelve Steps does not mean that Alcoholics Anonymous has reviewed or approved the contents of this publication, nor that AA agrees with the views expressed herein. The views expressed herein are solely those of the author. AA is a program of recovery from alcoholism. Use of the Twelve Steps in connection with programs and activities that are patterned after AA, but which address other problems, does not imply otherwise.

This isolation feeds the disease that is devouring us, even as it saps us of the will we need to begin our recovery by taking Step One.

This is where the "we" comes in. Other people who have found their way to Twelve Step fellowships have discovered not only how to become sober but how to recover from their isolation and despair.

> *Some people can stop drinking or using other drugs, and stay sober all by themselves. They can rely on their solitary "me." We can't.*

The First Step is an invitation to belong, because when you understand you are truly powerless, then all that remains is to become part of something bigger—a collective "we" that is eager to share its experiences of recovering from the deadly disease of addiction.

For people in recovery, helping others through the First Step and into the fellowship is a vital part of their own recovery program. Helping others find sobriety nourishes their own.

We are all in this together. As a member of the fellowship might say, "What worked for me might just work for you, so let me tell you about it."

The Basics of Addiction

Addiction, or substance use disorder, is a complex brain disease "characterized by compulsive drug seeking and continued use despite harmful consequences."*

Alcohol and other drugs change brain chemistry over time. These changes in the brain are the source of the negative symptoms people who develop an addiction experience, including intense cravings and the inability to stop using. If left untreated, these symptoms will only get worse.

Not everyone who uses addictive substances will develop substance use disorder. Millions of people use medication as prescribed and drink in moderation. Others misuse substances by drinking excessively, taking medication in ways other than as prescribed, or repeatedly using drugs to relieve stress or avoid reality—but are still able to stop whenever they want.

In contrast, a person with substance use disorder will find quitting physically and emotionally painful, and extremely difficult, particularly without professional help.

---

*National Institute on Drug Abuse. "Dear Journalist." NIDA, July 2, 2018. https://www.drugabuse.gov/publications/media-guide.

"Our Lives Had Become Unmanageable"

The possibility of reprieve that the First Step offers sounds like a relief. It's a miracle, in fact, when we think of what our lives were like before we came into recovery.

As we face the demands of the First Step, we have to face fundamental facts that we ignored while we slogged through another night, drunk or high, and awoke to another soul-sapping hangover—because of our use, our lives were unmanageable.

Those facts are simple: We have to take responsibility for ourselves, and we have to stop lying. Lying is a big component of the out-of-control life of those who are addicted to alcohol or other drugs. This may sound harsh, but it's important to consider the ways we lied when we were using alcohol or other drugs.

We lied to our partners:
> *"I only had a couple of beers—maybe three."*

We lied to our friends:
> *"I'm not going to drink tonight, so I can drive."*

We lied to our bosses:
> *"I can't make it in today—got this bug I just can't shake."*

We lied to our kids:
> *"Yeah, I promised I'd take you to the zoo, but I'm just too tired."*

We lied so often, so effortlessly, to cover up our drinking and using that it became as much a reflex as breathing. And then the lies became so unending that we began to believe them even as we spun more of them. The biggest lies are the ones we told ourselves:

> *"I can quit anytime I want."*
>
> *"I have this under control."*
>
> *"What I do to myself doesn't hurt anyone else."*
>
> *"I deserve a drink after the day I had."*
>
> *"Drinking hasn't caused me any real problems. I still have my . . . "*

This litany of lies means we didn't take responsibility for anything we did—or didn't do.

Are our lives unmanageable because a tornado tore through our neighborhood? Or because of an earthquake or hurricane or tsunami? All of us are powerless in those situations. We certainly weren't responsible for the weather. But we're lying again if we pretend we aren't responsible for our behavior while using. We spawned chaos, caused heartbreak, and reduced many lives—not just our own—to rubble.

Calling our lives unmanageable is a bland way of describing both the havoc alcohol or other drugs created in the many moments when we were under the influence *and* the wreckage our use of them left in their wake. Tornadoes and earthquakes can cause the same devastation, but our using is not a natural occurrence. *We've caused all this pain* because we've taken substances into our bodies that change our brain chemistry to the point that we have an incurable disease.

With no understanding of how substance use disorder develops, we may have consoled or defended ourselves with beliefs and excuses.

> "I've heard addiction is hereditary."
>
> "The daily pressures of my life are just too much to bear without a pick-me-up."
>
> "I love the way cocaine makes me feel."
>
> "Life is just too boring when I'm sober."

But the truth comes down to a simple admission: we lack the power on our own to control our drinking or use of other drugs.

It doesn't matter why we're powerless. At this point, accepting the fact that we are—finally leaving the defenses and lies behind—is all we need to do to begin the process of recovery by taking the First Step.

When we've finally accepted that we are powerless, we also have to accept the fact that the alcohol or other drugs are what made our lives so unmanageable. All those lies we told ourselves and others were gateways to even more lies that we came to believe because they let us continue to use.

> "My life is unmanageable, but it's because no one respects me."
>
> "The deck is stacked against me."
>
> "My husband doesn't understand me."
>
> "Life is unfair."

No, the truth is our lives have become unmanageable because *we have a disease* that hijacks our brain and may eventually kill us if untreated.

"We Were Powerless"

At some point, we could admit that our life was, indeed, out of control, but when we approached the other admission the First Step requires us to make, many of us balked.

> "Powerless? Who, me? Over something as trivial as drinking or using? The words sound nice, but do I really have to go that far? Can't I just manage it, get it under control if I really try this time?"

That voice we hear in these moments is our ego talking. And not just talking but fighting to survive, to not succumb to the idea that we are powerless. Our ego may have been shouting (or whispering) in our ears ever since addiction took hold of us. The ego pushes the "me, me, me" impulse that nurtures the belief we could get sober on our own, but why should we.

We've got this all under control! *Except that we don't. Not really.*

And so, more likely than not, we go on drinking or using again pretty much like we always did before, picking up where we have temporarily left off.

Do We Need to Know Why?

Burrowing into the "why" of our powerlessness won't get us anywhere closer to sobriety. It won't get us to the door of Step One or across its threshold and on the road to recovery. At this point, it really doesn't matter *why* we can't stop. And focusing too intently on the "why" is treacherous. It's our ego's way of giving the disease time to cause more damage and take deeper hold. It gives us an excuse to quit trying to get sober.

Maybe the best answer to why is that life is unfair. Many people *can* stop drinking or using. For them, they've had enough; when it comes to substances, they can take them or leave them. They get up from the table, leaving behind a half-full glass. Their stash is tucked under the bed for months.

For those of us with substance use disorder, it's never just one or two. Or every few months. Once is both never enough and too many. That's the only "why" we need to know.

Addiction Is a Disease

Few would claim that they have the power to beat a cancer that has invaded their body. Most know they cannot overpower their heart disease on their own. There's no magic cure for cancer or heart disease, which is why we submit to the care of those who can help us manage them. These diseases can be treated, and people often recover to live long, happy lives. The disease of addiction is no different.

Substance use disorder can't be cured, but it doesn't have to kill us either. We can recover. What we have to do is follow a treatment plan that works.

> *Proof that recovery is possible is as close as the nearest Twelve Step meeting. The people we meet there are the proof, and they are eager to let us know how it worked for them.*

How Stigma Threatens Recovery

Those of us with substance use disorder live daily with the social stigma of behavior that much of society sees as being selfish or showing a lack of willpower. As a result, many of us have learned to be deeply, deeply ashamed of ourselves. We punish ourselves for the pain we have inflicted and the wrongs we have committed. The resulting guilt and shame have been a barrier too high for some people to climb—a block to admitting powerlessness and asking for help. The effects of stigma have robbed many of recovery, and they've paid with their lives.

So of course we recoil at the thought of saying that we're powerless. The feelings of shame that we believe would accompany admitting to ourselves—much less everyone else—that we were unable or incompetent leave us weak at the knees and keep us firmly in the grasp of our deadly disease.

The Twelve Step fellowship challenges us to turn our back on the stigma we've been taught.

Among the things the First Step asks us to believe is that there's strength in admitting that sobriety is beyond our power to achieve on our own. The unstated promise of this Step is that, with the help of others, we can achieve sobriety and recovery.

Set the shame and guilt aside for now. If cancer patients shouldn't be ashamed of their disease, why should someone with substance use disorder? The task right now is to quit using; if you choose to follow the suggested Twelve Step program of recovery—a miracle that has worked for millions—you will have the time and support to face the sources and consequences of all of that shame and guilt in due time.

And So We Admitted . . .

It's easy to *say* we're powerless over alcohol or other drugs if we continue to more or less "manage" the wreck our lives have become. It's just as easy to *say* that our lives are unmanageable, even if we don't name our alcohol or other drug use as the reason. Yet we've discovered that half measures like these simply don't work. They give us an escape hatch back to drinking or using.

> *To take Step One completely and without reservations, we need to admit that we are powerless over our substance use and that this use has made our lives unmanageable.*

As you read this, by yourself, you may be left feeling this is just too hard, that it's asking you to accomplish the impossible. Sticking with the life you've got now would be easier, true. But the First Step is simple too. And it is a step away from your out-of-control life—a life of pain and desperation—into one where hope, healing, and joy can be found.

All by yourself, taking the First Step might be too hard, even impossible. But you don't have to take it by yourself.

As the first word of the First Step says, it is a life-saving choice you can make with the help of the Twelve Step fellowship— a community of recovering people who rely on the power of "we."

SUMMARY

If you want to get sober, if you want to quit, the First Step is a good start. If you want your life back, free from alcohol and other drugs, the Twelve Steps can show you the way to a new life.

Step One has been the beginning for millions of people who have embraced the fellowship of Alcoholics Anonymous and other Twelve Step groups. It can work for you, one step at a time. It all starts with the First Step.

TWELVE STEPS
OF ALCOHOLICS ANONYMOUS*

1. We admitted we were powerless over alcohol—that our lives had become unmanageable.

2. Came to believe that a Power greater than ourselves could restore us to sanity.

3. Made a decision to turn our will and our lives over to the care of God *as we understood Him.***

4. Made a searching and fearless moral inventory of ourselves.

5. Admitted to God, to ourselves, and to another human being the exact nature of our wrongs.

6. Were entirely ready to have God remove all these defects of character.

7. Humbly asked Him to remove our shortcomings.

8. Made a list of all persons we had harmed, and became willing to make amends to them all.

9. Made direct amends to such people wherever possible, except when to do so would injure them or others.

10. Continued to take personal inventory and when we were wrong promptly admitted it.

11. Sought through prayer and meditation to improve our conscious contact with God *as we understood Him*, praying only for knowledge of His will for us and the power to carry that out.

12. Having had a spiritual awakening as the result of these steps, we tried to carry this message to alcoholics, and to practice these principles in all our affairs.

---

* Taken from *Alcoholics Anonymous*, 4th ed., published by Alcoholics Anonymous World Services, Inc., New York, NY, pages 59-60. Reprinted with permission of Alcoholics Anonymous World Services, Inc.

** In AA recovery, "God" is gender neutral. While the Steps as they appear here are directly from the AA Big Book, this phrase is often spoken and written as "God as we understood God."

MY NOTES

MY NOTES

MY NOTES